Giant Anteaters

by Samantha Seiple and Todd Seiple

 Lerner Publications Company • Minneapolis

For Ben Powlus

The photographs in this book are used with the permission of: © SA Team/Foto Natura/ Minden Pictures, pp. 4, 10; © P. Oxford/Peter Arnold, Inc., p. 6; © Bruce Davidson/ naturepl.com, p. 7; © Pete Oxford/naturepl.com, pp. 8, 16, 20, 32, 35, 47; © Heinz Plenge/ Peter Arnold, Inc., p. 9; © ZSSD/SuperStock, pp. 11, 12 (right); © kevinschafer.com, pp. 12 (left), 34; © Luiz C. Marigo/Peter Arnold, Inc., pp. 13, 23, 25; © age fotostock/SuperStock, pp. 14, 15, 17, 33, 39; © Pete Oxford/Minden Pictures/Getty Images, pp. 18, 22, 43; © Tom Brakefield/CORBIS, pp. 19, 21, 46; © Tony Linck/SuperStock, p. 24; © Roland Seitre/Peter Arnold, Inc., p. 26; © Theo Allofs/Visuals Unlimited, p. 27; © Wegner, P./Peter Arnold, Inc., p. 28; © Andreas Meier/Reuters/CORBIS, p. 29; © Singapore Night Safari/epa/CORBIS, p. 30; © Joel Sartore/National Geographic/Getty Images, p. 31; © Rod Williams/naturepl.com, p. 36; © Scott Barbour/Getty Images, pp. 37, 42; © Victor Englebert/Time & Life Pictures/Getty Images, p. 38; © Frans Lanting/Minden Pictures, p. 40; © Therin-Weise/Peter Arnold, Inc., p. 41; © Joe McDonald/CORBIS, p. 48 (top); © iStockphoto.com/Michael Chen, p. 48 (bottom).

Cover: © Theo Allofs/CORBIS.

Text copyright © 2008 by Lerner Publishing Group, Inc.

Lerner Publications Company
A division of Lerner Publishing Group, Inc.
241 First Avenue North
Minneapolis, MN 55401 U.S.A.

Website address: www.lernerbooks.com

Library of Congress Cataloging-in-Publication Data

Seiple, Samantha.
    Giant anteaters / by Samantha Seiple and Todd Seiple.
        p.   cm. — (Early bird nature books)
    Includes index.
    ISBN-13: 978–0–8225–7887–1 (lib. bdg. : alk. paper)
    1. Myrmecophaga—Juvenile literature. I. Seiple, Todd.
II. Title.
QL737.E24S45 2008
599.3'14—dc22   2007024881

Manufactured in the United States of America
1 2 3 4 5 6 – JR – 13 12 11 10 09 08

Contents

Giant anteaters live in Central and South America. The striped area shows where giant anteaters live.

Be a Word Detective

Can you find these words as you read about giant anteaters? Be a detective and try to figure out what they mean. You can turn to the glossary on page 46 for help.

diurnal

extinct

insectivores

insects

habitats

knuckle walking

mammals

nocturnal

nursing

predators

proboscis

rain forests

reserve

territory

Chapter 1

This giant anteater has found a meal. What body part do giant anteaters use to find food?

Giant Anteaters Are Not Aardvarks

Ants scurry to and from their mound. They are hard at work. Suddenly, a long tongue snaps out of a tubelike snout. It is the tongue and snout of a giant anteater. It has found its favorite food. Ants!

Giant anteaters are unusual-looking animals. But their bodies are perfect for eating ants and other insects. A giant anteater has a long snout called a proboscis (pruh-BAHS-kuhs). It uses its proboscis to smell. A giant anteater's sense of smell is 40 times more powerful than yours. Giant anteaters can easily smell ants, termites, and other tiny insects.

A giant anteater has a very keen sense of smell. To find food, the anteater follows its snout.

Giant anteaters have small ears and eyes. Scientists are not sure if giant anteaters have excellent or poor hearing. But they do know that giant anteaters cannot see very well. So giant anteaters use their proboscises to help guide them.

A giant anteater has one eye and one ear on each side of its head.

Inside a giant anteater's proboscis is a purple tongue. It looks like a long worm. It is about 24 inches long. A human's tongue is about 4 inches long. A giant anteater's long tongue helps it reach insects that are hiding.

A giant anteater's long tongue is thick near the top and narrow at the tip.

A giant anteater has a small mouth at the end of its proboscis. The opening is the size of a nickel. That is just large enough for the tongue to go in and out. A giant anteater does not have any teeth in its mouth.

A giant anteater takes a drink of water.

An aardvark eats ants and termites, just like giant anteaters do. But giant anteaters are not related to aardvarks.

Giant anteaters belong to a group of mammals that have few or no teeth. Mammals are animals that have hair and feed their babies milk. Some people think anteaters look like mammals called aardvarks. But aardvarks have peglike teeth that grow their whole lives. They are not anteaters. The closest relatives of anteaters are sloths and armadillos.

Pygmy anteaters (left) *have brownish, silky hair. The hair on this tamandua* (right) *is white and black.*

The giant anteater is one kind of anteater. The pygmy anteater and the tamandua (tuh-MAN-duh-wuh) are other kinds. They are much smaller than giant anteaters. They also have shorter proboscises and thinner tails. They use their thin tails to hang and swing from trees. Giant anteaters live on the ground. They are the biggest of the anteaters. They are the size of large dogs.

A giant anteater has a thick coat of hair. It feels like straw. The fur is black, brown, gray, and white. Two black-and-white stripes run down a giant anteater's back. The different colors help the anteater blend in with its surroundings.

A giant anteater's hair helps it hide in tall grass and bushes. Its thick hair also protects it from insect bites.

A giant anteater has a bushy tail. It uses its tail as a blanket when it sleeps. A giant anteater also uses its tail to help it stand up on its two back legs.

This sleepy giant anteater has curled up for a nap.

Giant anteaters walk on all four feet. Can you see the claws on this giant anteater's front foot?

When giant anteaters walk, they shuffle their feet. This is because their front claws are very sharp and long. Giant anteaters cannot pull in their claws the way cats can. So giant anteaters turn their claws inward and make fists. Then they walk on the backs of their paws. This is called knuckle walking. Knuckle walking protects giant anteaters' claws and keeps them sharp.

Giant anteaters walk slowly. It takes a giant anteater two hours to walk 1 mile. A human could walk 6 miles in that amount of time. But giant anteaters can run fast for short distances. If the fastest human raced a giant anteater in the 100-yard dash, the giant anteater would win by almost 1 second. In other words, the giant anteater would win by a nose.

A giant anteater speeds away from danger. Some giant anteaters can run 31 miles an hour!

A giant anteater makes its way through some water.

Giant anteaters are excellent swimmers. When an anteater swims underwater, it can use its proboscis as a snorkel. It sticks its proboscis out of the water and breathes the air above the surface. Then the giant anteater can swim far with just its snout sticking out for air.

Chapter 2

A giant anteater sniffs a termite mound. How will the giant anteater reach the insects inside?

Ants, Ants, and More Ants

Giant anteaters are insectivores (ihn-SEHK-tuh-vorz). Insectivores are animals that eat insects. Giant anteaters like to eat soft and juicy carpenter ants. They try to stay away from insects with strong jaws, such as soldier ants. Insects with strong jaws can bite the anteaters.

A giant anteater uses its proboscis to search for ants and termites in logs or mounds. The anteater tears open the insects' nests with its sharp claws. Its long tongue flicks in and out more than 150 times a minute. When the giant anteater eats, its tongue becomes coated in gluelike saliva. Saliva is spit. The sticky saliva covers the insects. It also picks up thousands of eggs and young insects.

A giant anteater uses its claws to tear open a log where insects live.

Since giant anteaters are toothless, they cannot bite or chew their food. Instead, a giant anteater crushes the insects against the roof of its mouth. The anteater also uses the muscles in its stomach to further break down the food.

A giant anteater sits down for a quick meal from a termite mound.

A giant anteater can eat up to 30,000 insects in one day!
This giant anteater is licking insects off the leaves of bushes.

A giant anteater eats for only a few minutes at a time. Then it looks for insects somewhere else. The giant anteater lets some of the insects in each spot live. If the anteater returns to one of the spots later, there will still be some insects to eat. And eating for only a few minutes at a time keeps the giant anteater from being bitten by too many insects.

Chapter 3

A giant anteater walks through a field alone. Where do giant anteaters live?

Lone Wanderers

The places where giant anteaters live are called their habitats (HAB-uh-tats). Giant anteaters live in several habitats. They can be found in rain forests, swampy areas, and grasslands in Central and South America.

Giant anteaters wander from place to place. They do not have permanent homes or nests. But they do stay within a large area of land called a territory. They hunt for insects in their territory. When giant anteaters want to sleep, they find a new spot in their territory.

A giant anteater wanders through its territory. What kind of habitat is it in?

Giant anteaters prefer to sleep in bushes, logs, and underground homes left by other animals. This giant anteater found a spot under a tree.

Giant anteaters sleep up to 16 hours each day. They are light sleepers and are easily startled awake. In the countryside, giant anteaters are diurnal (dy-UR-nuhl). This means they are awake during the day. Giant anteaters that live in areas near people are nocturnal (nahk-TUR-nuhl). This means giant anteaters are awake at night and asleep during the day.

Giant anteaters live alone. They do not typically live with other giant anteaters. If a giant anteater spots another giant anteater, it will ignore the other anteater or run away. If giant anteaters feel in danger, their hair will stand on end. This makes them look bigger and scarier to other animals.

The hair on a giant anteater's back sticks up when it smells an enemy nearby.

Sometimes, a fight breaks out between two giant anteaters. The anteaters will tuck in their claws. Then they circle and push each other. They snort, sniff, hiss, and roar. But giant anteaters try to avoid deadly fights.

A giant anteater gets ready to defend itself against an enemy.

Jaguars hunt and eat giant anteaters.

Giant anteaters also have to protect themselves from predators. Predators are animals that hunt and eat other animals. Jaguars and mountain lions kill giant anteaters for food. If a giant anteater comes across a predator, it stands up on its back legs and tail. Then the anteater uses its sharp claws to slash at the predator. Giant anteaters have strong legs too. They can crush an attacker by squeezing it with their legs.

Chapter 4

A mother with her baby takes a drink from the water. What is a baby giant anteater called?

Baby Giant Anteaters

A female giant anteater has her first baby when she is about two and a half years old. She looks for thick bushes or another safe place. Then she stands on her back legs and gives birth. A giant anteater usually has only one baby at a time. But sometimes twins are born.

A baby giant anteater is called a pup. A pup weighs about 3 pounds when it is born. That is as much as a newborn piglet.

A pup crawls onto its mother's back right after it is born.

A two-month-old pup clings to its mother.

A pup looks like a tiny grown-up anteater. It is born with a full coat of hair and two black-and-white stripes. A pup has sharp claws too.

A pup is raised by its mother. For the first six months, the pup drinks its mother's milk. This is called nursing. The pup will nurse for up to one hour at a time throughout the day.

This pup has lost its mother. It drinks milk from a bottle instead.

A giant anteater teaches her pup where to find food.

When the pup stops nursing, the mother helps the pup find ants and insects to eat. The pup learns to drink water by licking wet plants and fruit. The pup grows bigger and stronger.

The pup plays with its mother. It crawls all over her and tries to wrestle. The pup can also run slowly after one month. But it stays near its mother.

A pup licks its mother's fur.

The pup prefers to ride on its mother's back for the first year. The pup's coat of hair matches its mother's hair. So predators do not see the tiny pup on its mother's back. The mother also appears bigger to predators. So they stay away.

A baby anteater stays safe on its mother's back. When their stripes line up, the pup is hard to see. Can you spot the pup?

A giant anteater protects her pup while it eats.

Usually giant anteaters are very quiet. But when a pup is in danger or scared, it will call out to its mother. A pup's voice sounds like a high-pitched squeal.

After two years, a giant anteater is fully grown. Then it will leave its mother and live alone. Giant anteaters live about 15 years.

This female giant anteater is old enough to have babies of her own.

Chapter 5

People study giant anteaters to learn more about them. About how many giant anteaters live in the wild?

Giant Anteaters and People

Giant anteaters are near threatened. This means they could become extinct (ehk-STINGKT) someday. Then there would be no giant anteaters left on Earth. In 2006, there were only about 5,000 giant anteaters in the wild.

Some groups of people who live in the rain forests hunt and eat giant anteaters.

People cause the most problems for giant anteaters. Some farmers and ranchers think giant anteaters attack their dogs and cattle. So they kill the giant anteaters. People also hunt giant anteaters for food. Other hunters kill anteaters for sport. They display the dead anteaters in their homes. People catch giant anteaters to sell as pets too.

People can also harm the habitats of giant anteaters. People want to build new houses, roads, and towns. They also want more grassland for their cattle. People set fires in forests to clear away the trees. But giant anteaters have poor eyesight and are slow moving. Many of them die because they cannot escape the fires.

Fires in the rain forest kill many plants and animals that live there.

Some giant anteaters end up living near cities, towns, and busy roads. Sometimes, people accidentally run over the animals with their cars. In Brazil, signs warn drivers of giant anteaters crossing the road.

Signs like this one let drivers know that giant anteaters might cross the road to get to the other side.

This giant anteater lives in a park in South America. In the park, it is safe from hunters and other dangers.

Many people are trying to help giant anteaters. Countries in Central and South America have set up reserves. A reserve is an area of land. Animals that live in a reserve are protected. No one is allowed to kill animals on a reserve.

This pup was born in a zoo in London, England.

Zoos also try to protect giant anteaters. About 200 giant anteaters are in zoos around the world. Giant anteater pups are born in zoos every year. Zookeepers study what the anteaters do. Zookeepers teach other people about giant anteaters and how to protect them.

Giant anteaters have an important job in nature. And they are perfectly suited for it. Giant anteaters help control the number of ants and other insects. Without them, there would be too many bugs!

A giant anteater checks a tree trunk for insects.

LEARN MORE ABOUT
GIANT ANTEATERS

BOOKS

Aloian, Molly, and Bobbie Kalman. *Explore South America*. New York: Crabtree Publishing, 2007. Read about the landforms, places, people, animals, and plants of South America.

Dyer, Hadley, and Bobbie Kalman. *The Life Cycle of an Ant*. New York: Crabtree Publishing, 2005. Learn about ants, their habitats, and their life cycle.

Johnson, Rebecca L. *A Walk in the Rain Forest*. Minneapolis: Carolrhoda Books, 2001. Discover the plants, animals, sights, and sounds of the rain forests of North and Central America.

Squire, Ann O. *Anteaters, Sloths, and Armadillos*. New York: Franklin Watts, 1999. Read this introduction to the lives of anteaters and their relatives.

WEBSITES

Kids' Planet
http://www.kidsplanet.org
This website has information and activities on endangered animals, including armadillos and other South American animals.

Kratts' Creatures/PBS GO
http://pbskids.org/krattscreatures/flash.shtml
Check out games, video clips, and facts about giant anteaters and other wild animals on the Kratts brothers' website.

The Online Anteater
http://www.maiaw.com/anteater
Find anteater facts, photos, and cartoons and a list of zoos that have giant anteaters.

GLOSSARY

diurnal (dy-UR-nuhl): active during the daytime

extinct (ehk-STINGKT): no members of a kind of animal are still living

insectivores (ihn-SEHK-tuh-vorz): animals that eat insects

insects: animals with six legs and three main body parts. Most insects also have wings.

habitats (HAB-uh-tats): the places where a kind of animal can live and grow

knuckle walking: walking on the back of the paws or hands

mammals: a group of animals with warm blood and backbones. Mammals have hair and feed their young milk. Giant anteaters, people, and cows are mammals.

nocturnal (nahk-TUR-nuhl): active during the night

nursing: drinking mother's milk

predators: animals that hunt other animals for food

proboscis (pruh-BAHS-kuhs): a long snout

rain forests: warm, thick forests where a lot of rain falls

reserve: an area of land that is set aside to protect wild animals

territory: the area of land where a giant anteater wanders and hunts

INDEX

Pages listed in **bold** type refer to photographs.